Cursive HANDWRITING book *for* Kids

This Book Belongs To

A a

Apple

a a a a

a a a a

a a a a

a a a a

a a a a

a a a a

a a a a

B b

Bowl

B B B B

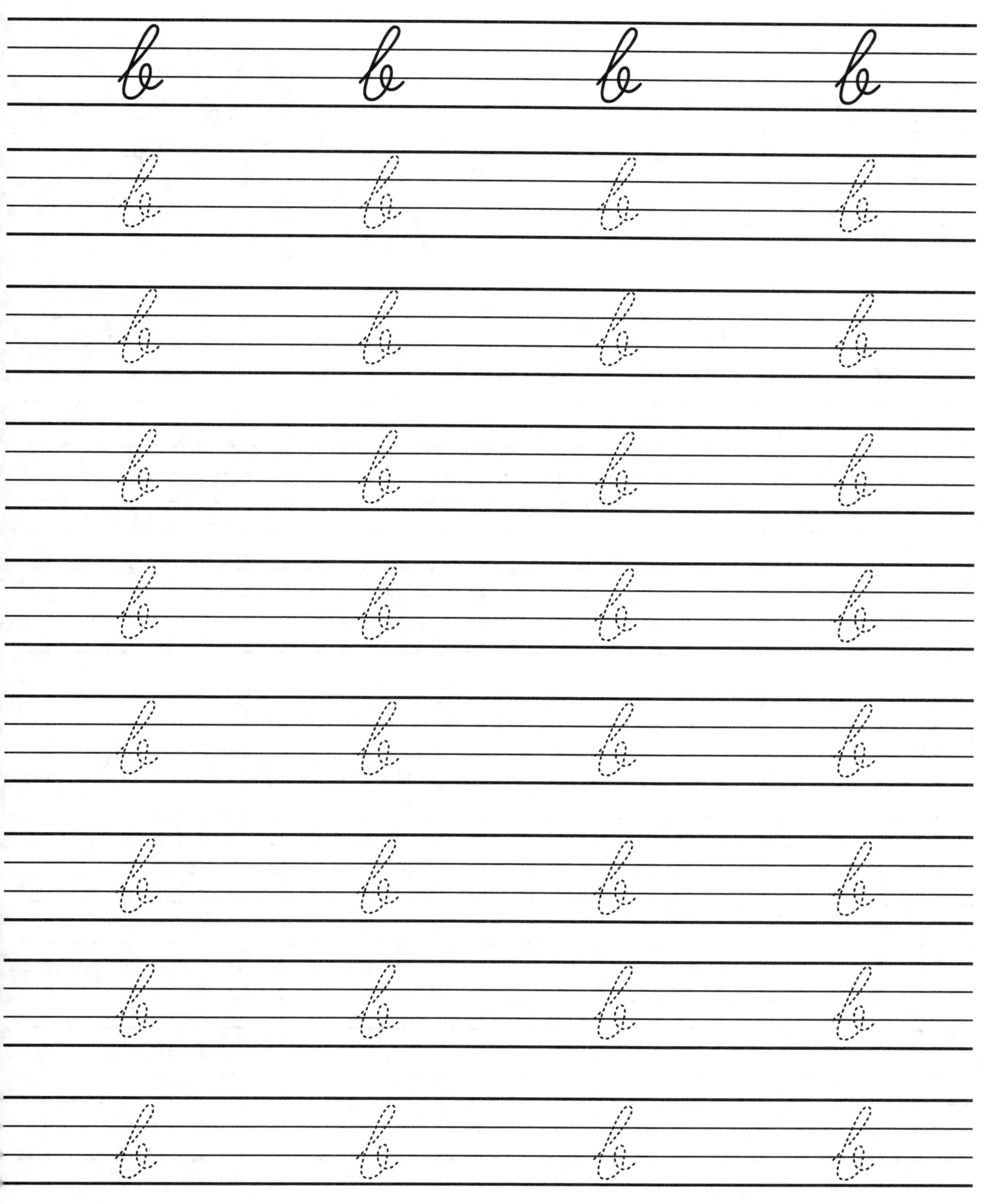

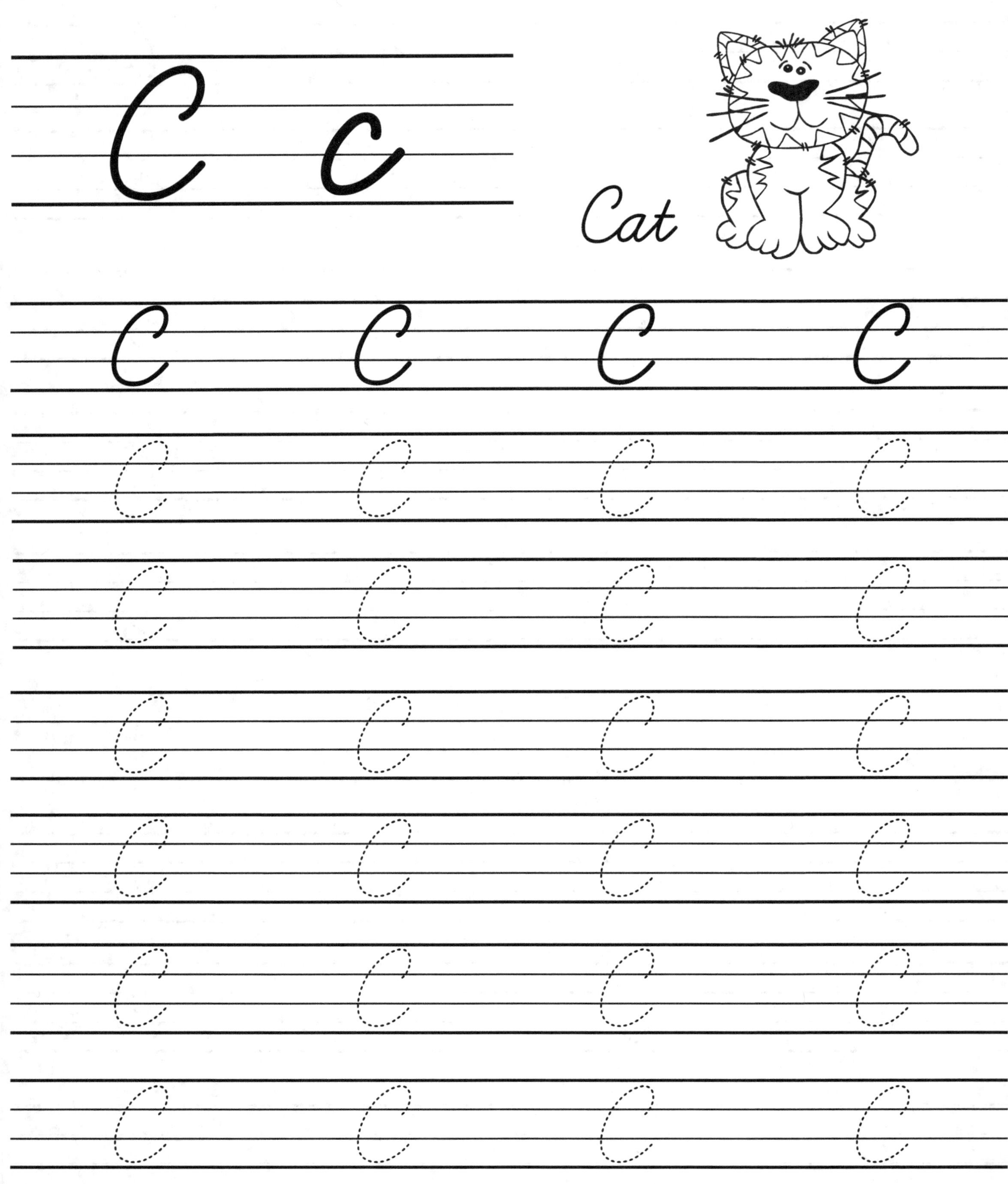
C c
Cat
C C C C

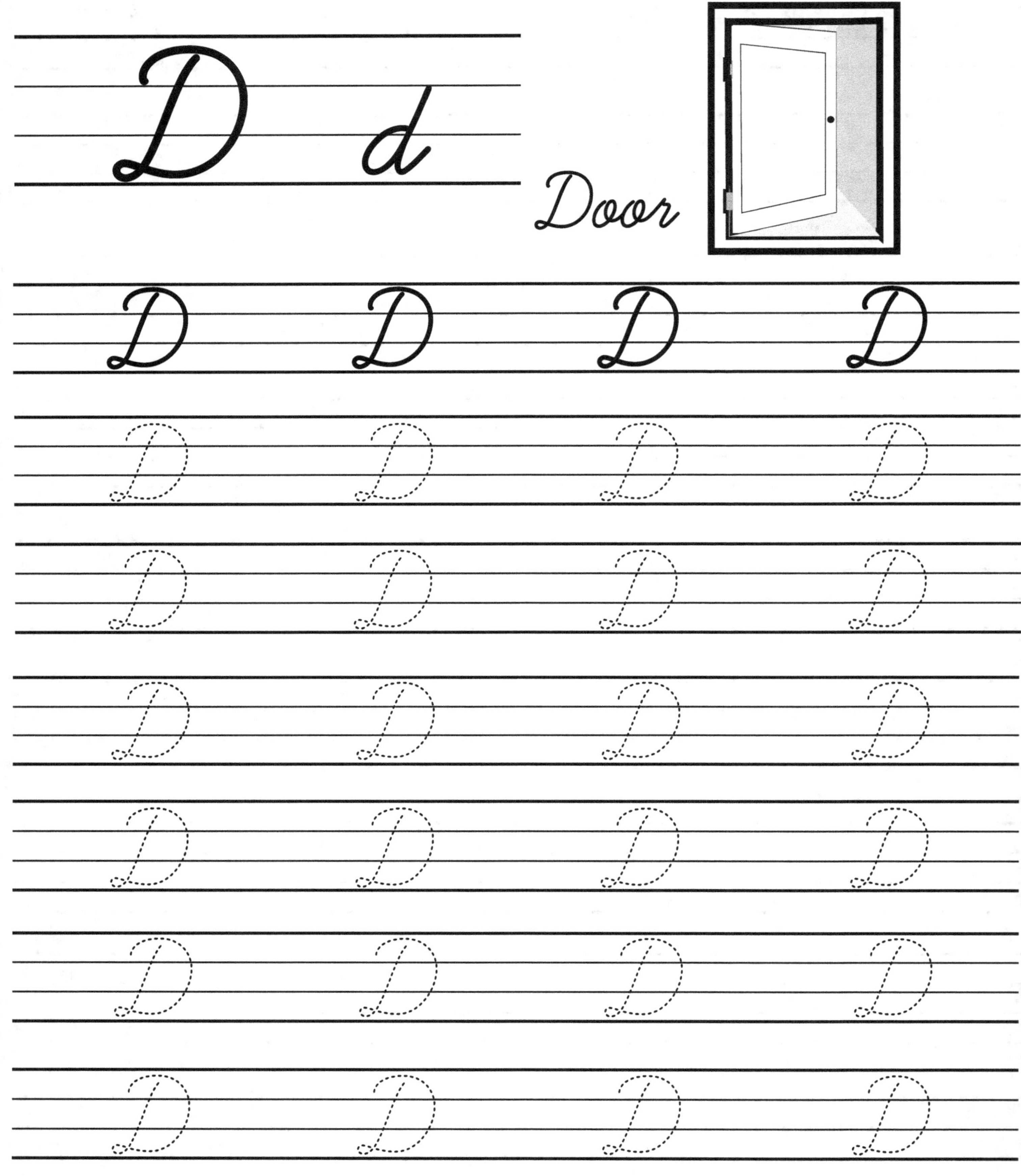

D d
Door

d d d d

d d d d

d d d d

d d d d

d d d d

d d d d

d d d d

d d d d

d d d d

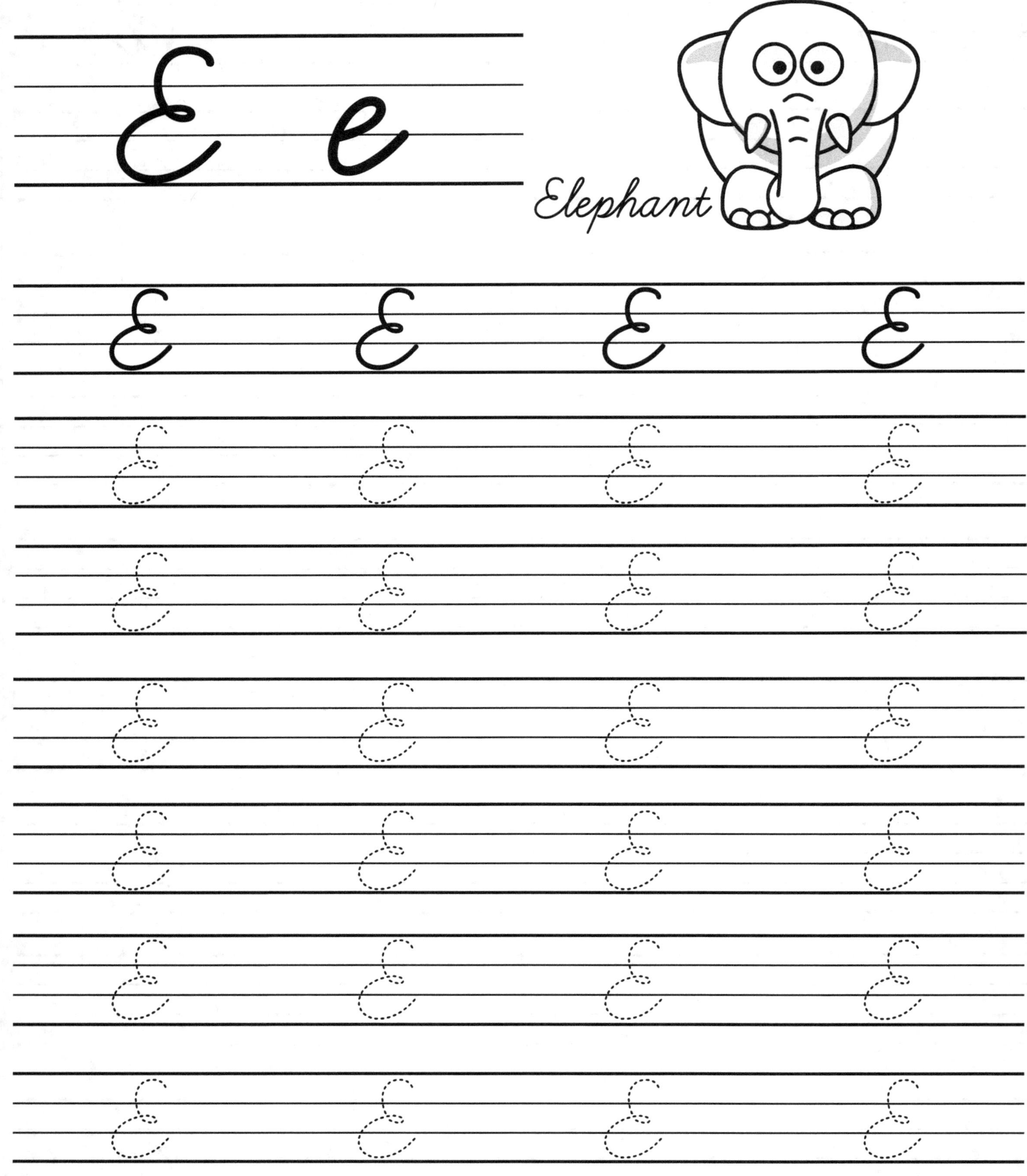

E e
Elephant

F f
Fox
F F F F

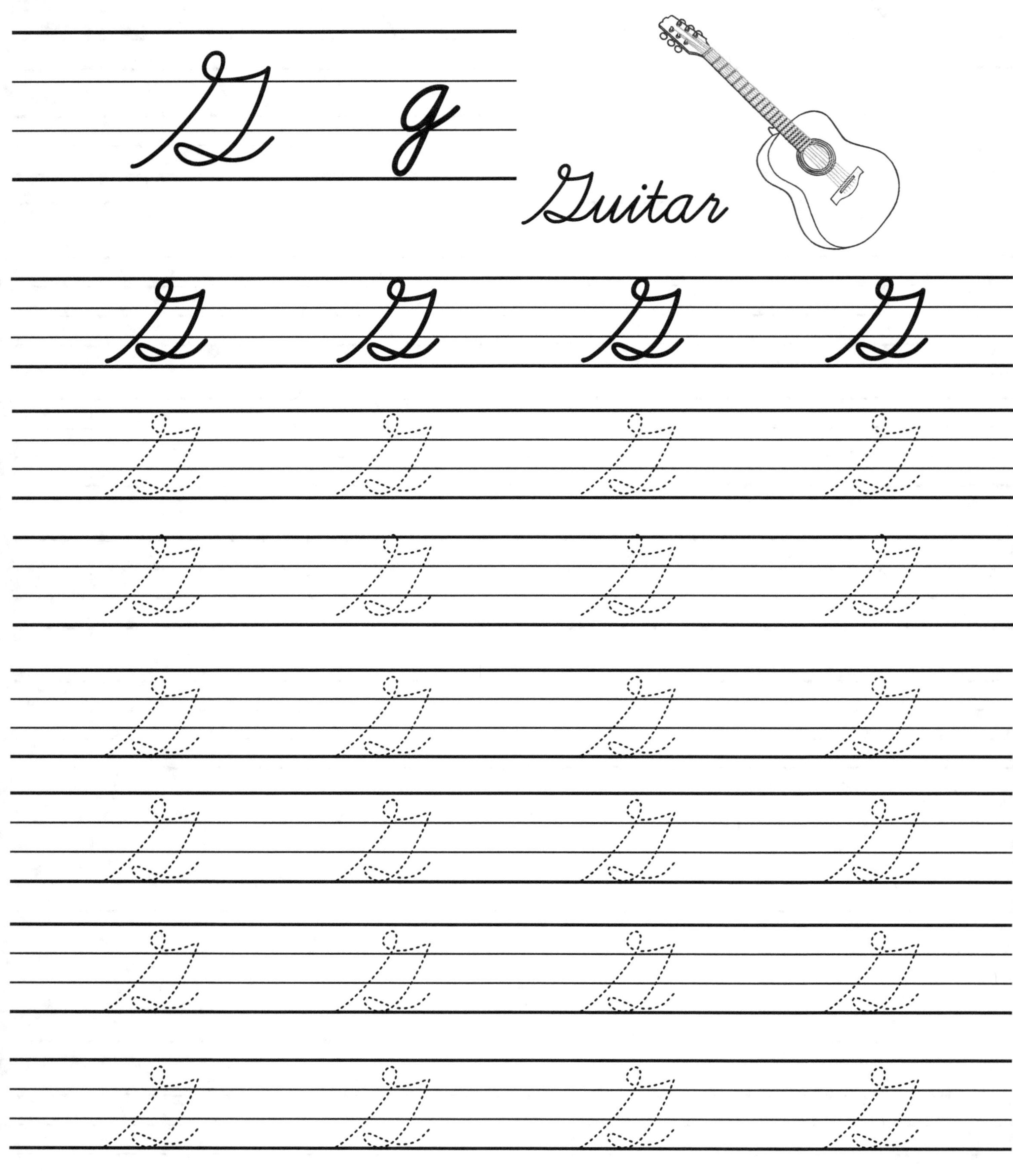
G g
Guitar

H h

House

H H H H

H H H H

H H H H

H H H H

H H H H

H H H H

H H H H

h h h h

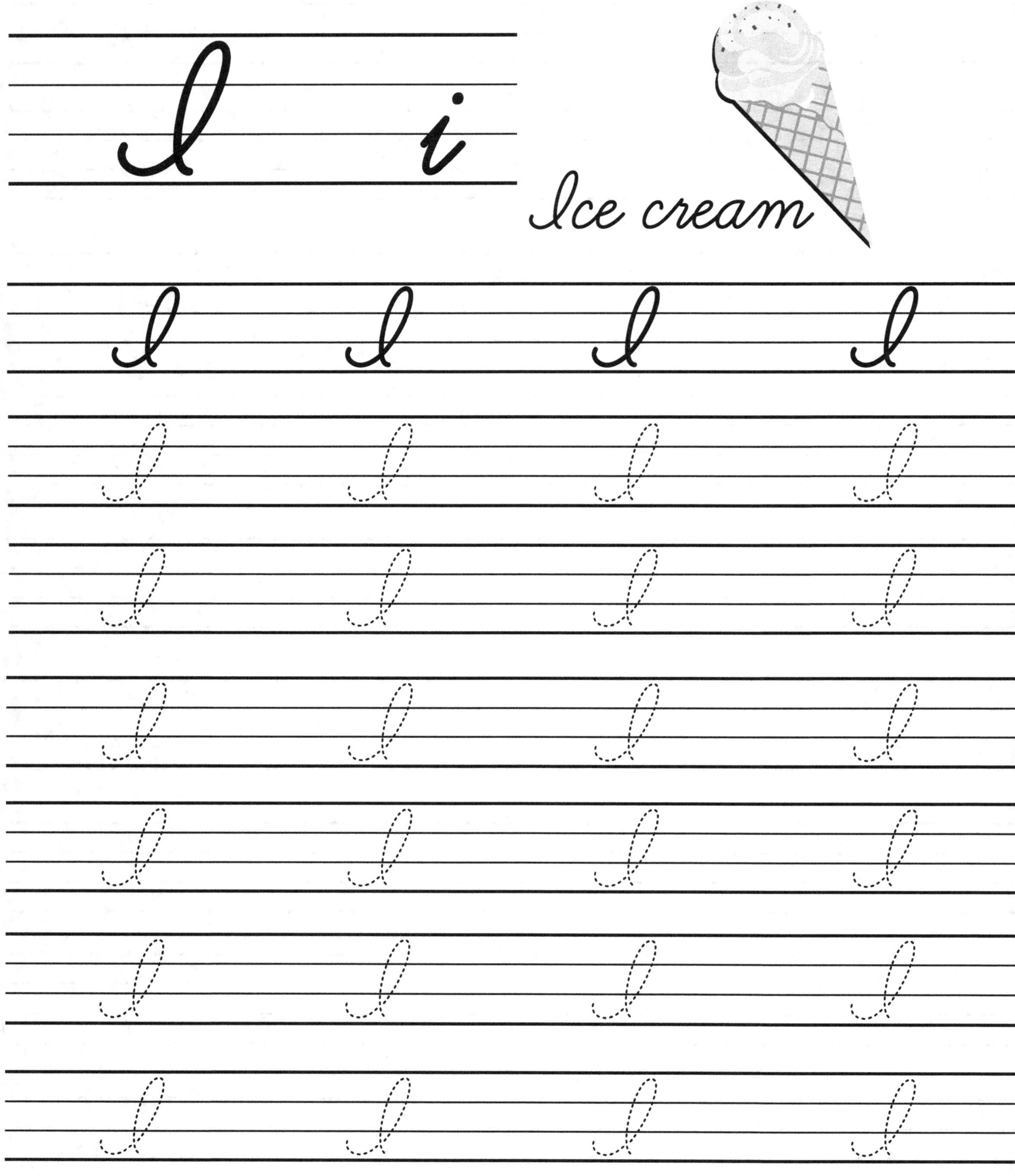
I i
Ice cream

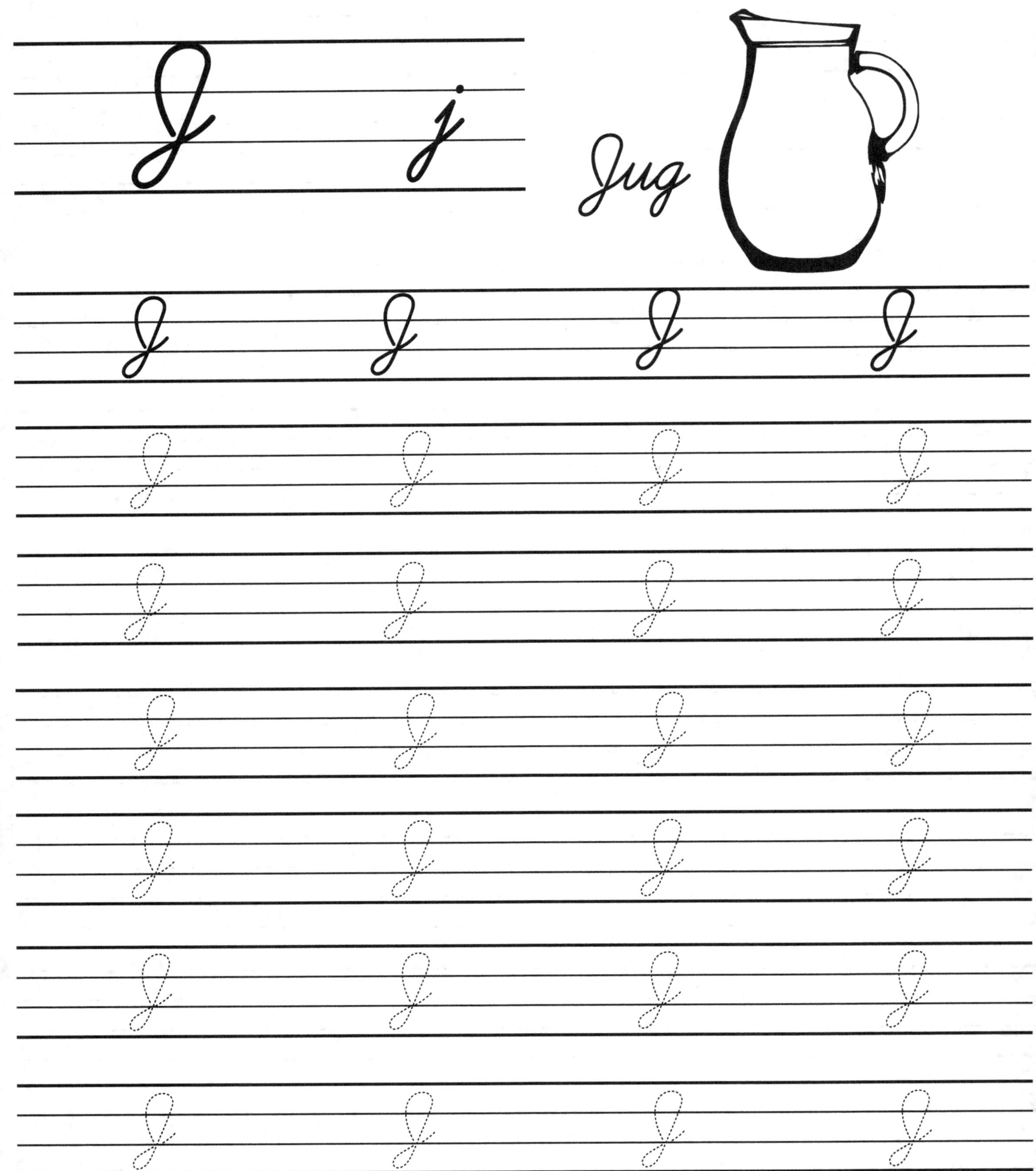
J j
Jug

K k

Kettle

K K K K

K K K K

K K K K

K K K K

K K K K

K K K K

K K K K

L l
Lion

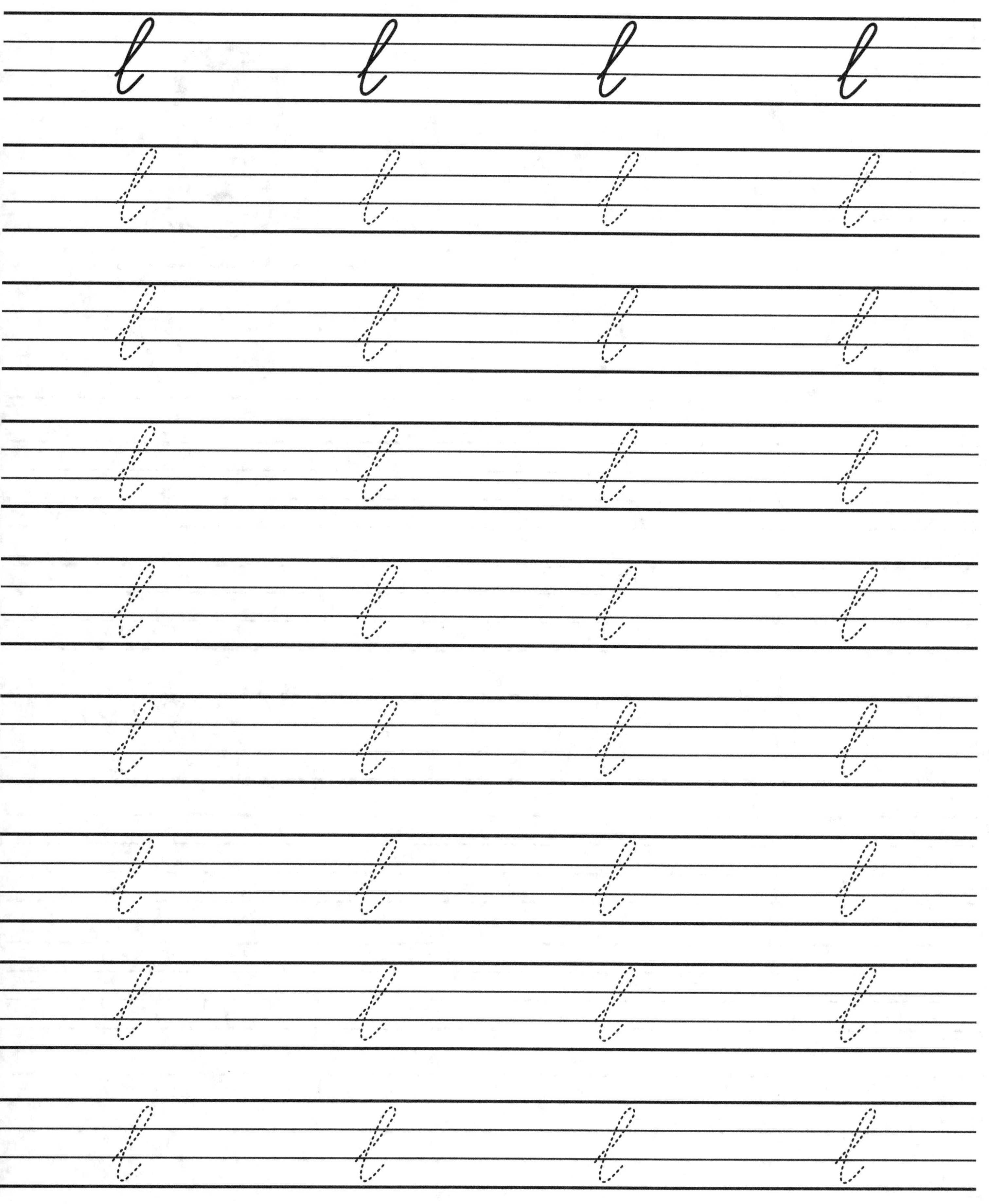

Mm Man

m m m m

m m m m

m m m m

m m m m

m m m m

m m m m

m m m m

m m m m

m m m m

m m m m

m m m m

m m m m

m m m m

m m m m

m m m m

m m m m

m m m m

N n

Nest

n n n n

n n n n

n n n n

n n n n

n n n n

n n n n

n n n n

n n n n

n n n n

n n n n

n n n n

n n n n

n n n n

n n n n

n n n n

n n n n

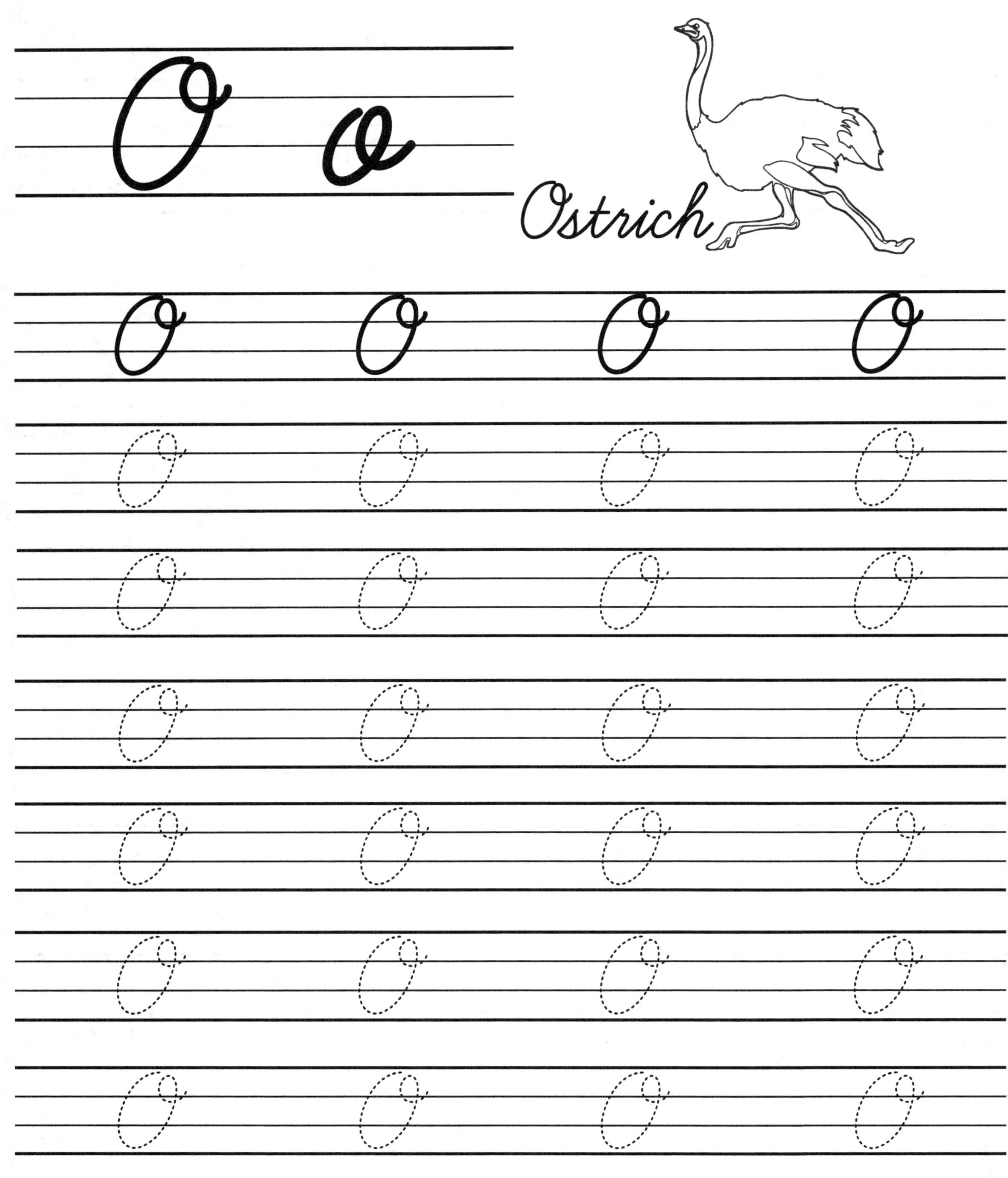
O o
Ostrich

P p

Paddle

p p p p

p p p p

p p p p

p p p p

p p p p

p p p p

p p p p

p p p p

Q q
Queen

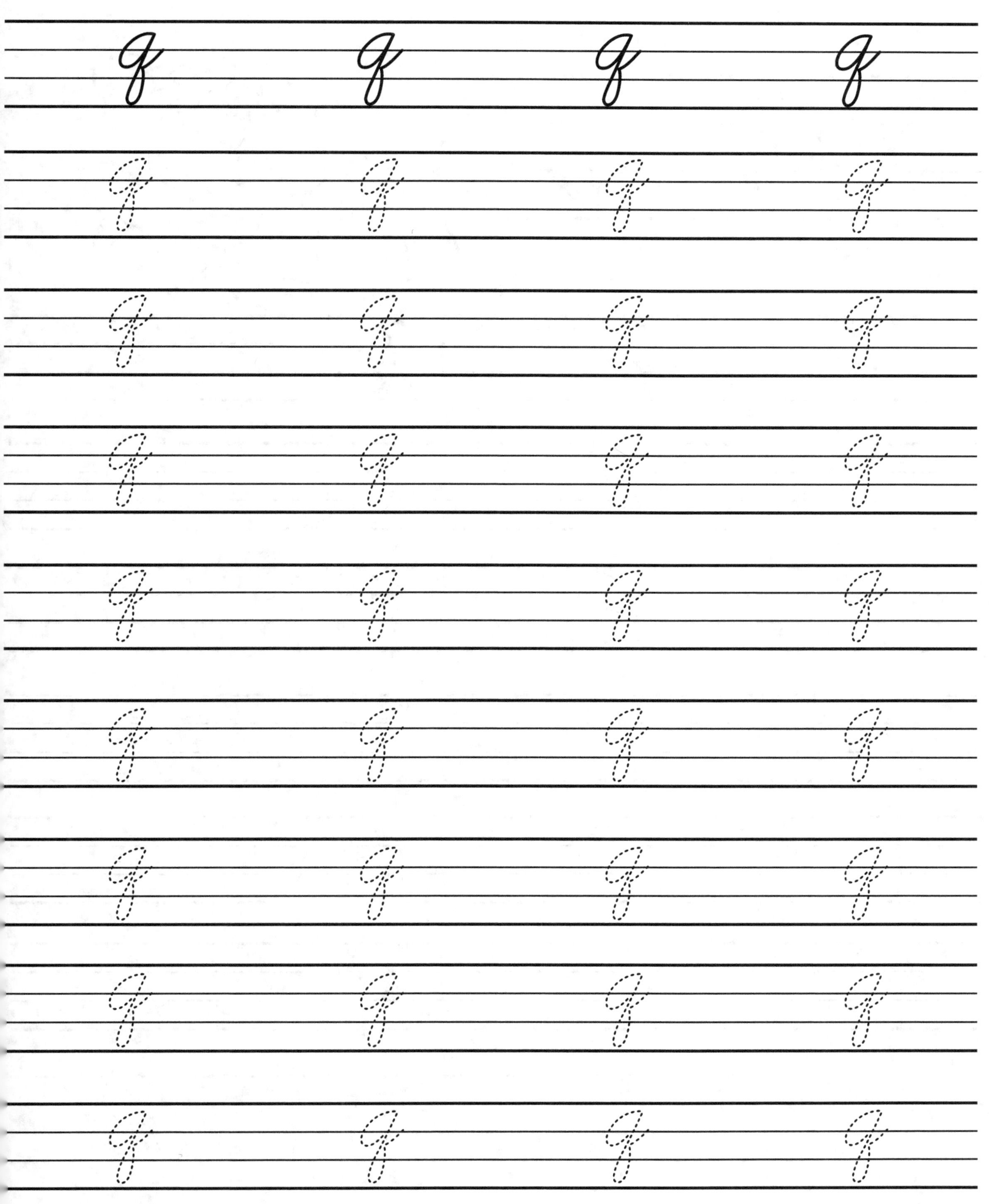

R r

Rose

R R R R

R R R R

R R R R

R R R R

R R R R

R R R R

R R R R

r r r r

r r r r

r r r r

r r r r

r r r r

r r r r

r r r r

r r r r

r r r r

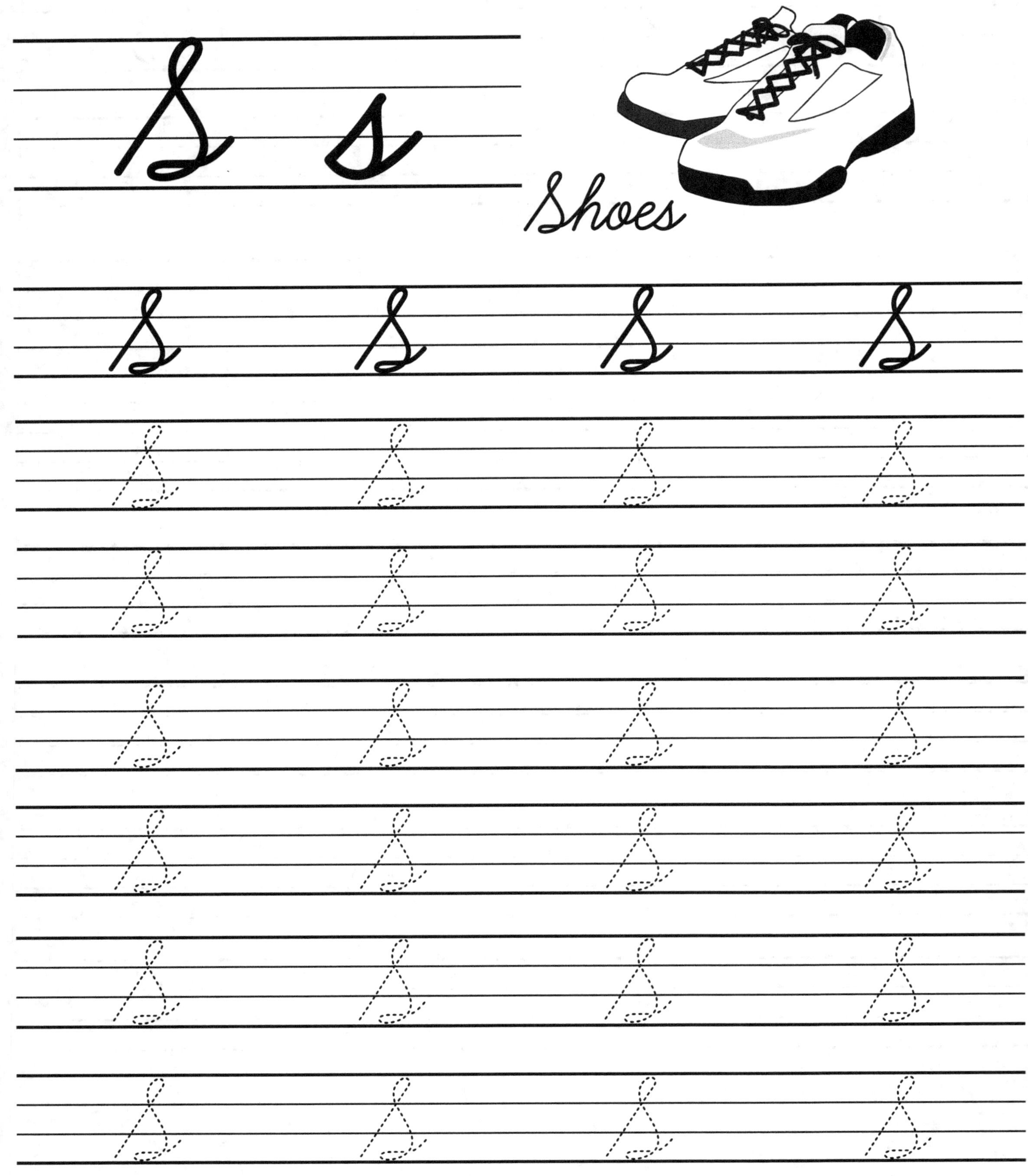
S s
Shoes

T t

Table

T T T T

t t t t

t t t t

t t t t

t t t t

t t t t

t t t t

t t t t

t t t t

t t t t

U u

Umbrella

U U U U

u u u u

u u u u

u u u u

u u u u

u u u u

u u u u

u u u u

u u u u

u u u u

V v
Van

u u u u

u u u u

u u u u

u u u u

u u u u

u u u u

u u u u

u u u u

u u u u

u u u u

W w

Wood

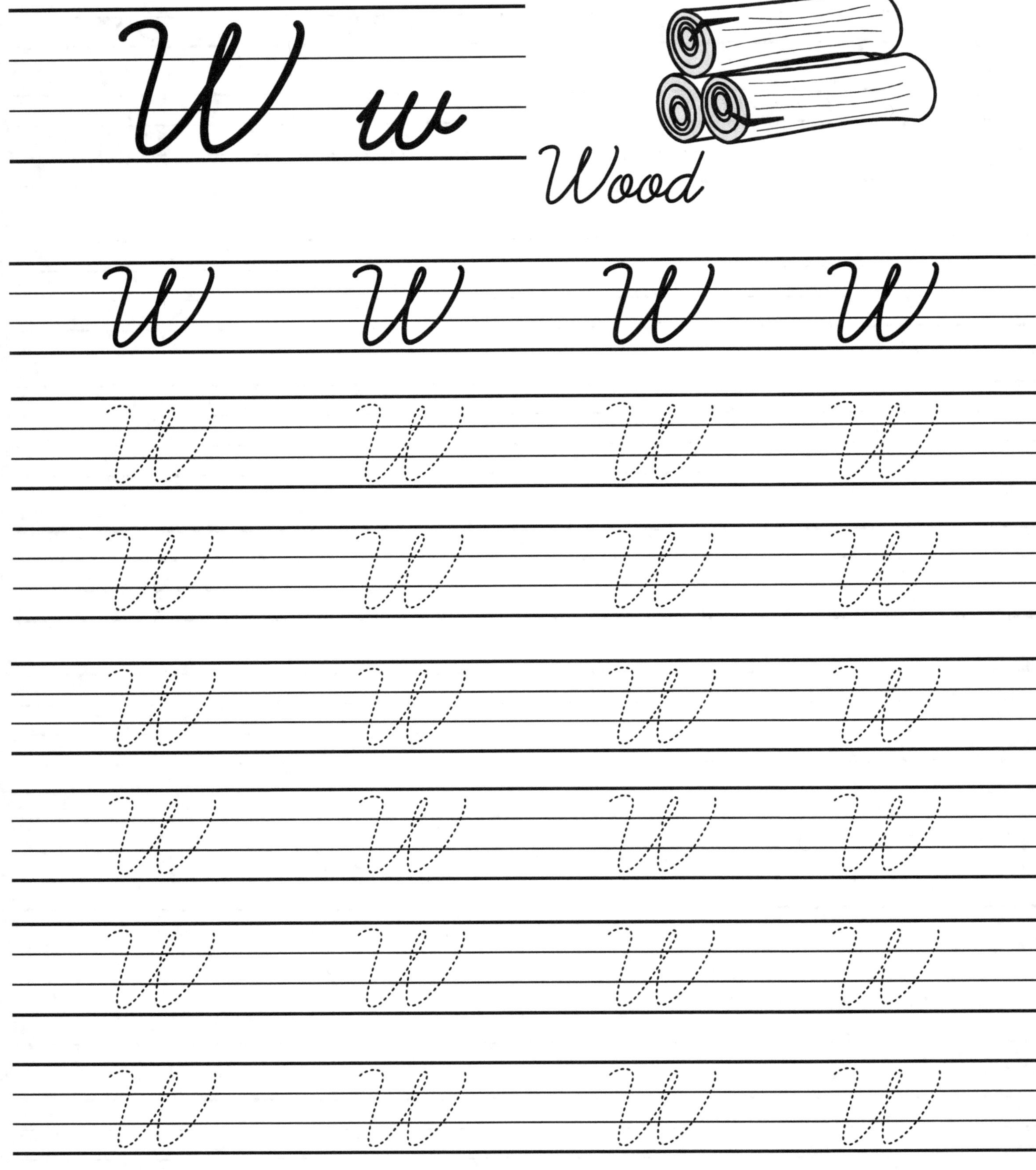

w w w w

w w w w

w w w w

w w w w

w w w w

w w w w

w w w w

w w w w

w w w w

w w w w

X x

Xylophone

X X X X

X X X X

X X X X

X X X X

X X X X

X X X X

X X X X

X X X X

X X X X

X X X X

X X X X

Y y
Yoyo
Y Y Y Y

y y y y

y y y y

y y y y

y y y y

y y y y

y y y y

y y y y

y y y y

y y y y

y y y y

Z z
Zip

as as as as

as as as as

as as as as

as as as as

as as as as

as as as as

as as as as

as as as as

as as as as

an an an an

an an an an

an an an an

an an an an

an an an an

an an an an

an an an an

an an an an

an an an an

am am am am

am am am am

am am am am

am am am am

am am am am

am am am am

am am am am

am am am am

am am am am

be be be be

be be be be

be be be be

be be be be

be be be be

be be be be

be be be be

be be be be

be be be be

by by by by

by by by by

by by by by

by by by by

by by by by

by by by by

by by by by

by by by by

by by by by

so so so so

so so so so

so so so so

so so so so

so so so so

so so so so

so so so so

so so so so

so so so so

or or or or

or or or or

or or or or

or or or or

or or or or

or or or or

or or or or

or or or or

or or or or

or or or or

to to to to

to to to to

to to to to

to to to to

to to to to

to to to to

to to to to

to to to to

to to to to

of of of of

in in in in

in in in in

in in in in

in in in in

in in in in

in in in in

in in in in

in in in in

in in in in

is *is* *is* *is*

is *is* *is* *is*

is *is* *is* *is*

is *is* *is* *is*

is *is* *is* *is*

is *is* *is* *is*

is *is* *is* *is*

is *is* *is* *is*

is *is* *is* *is*

it it it it

it it it it

it it it it

it it it it

it it it it

it it it it

it it it it

it it it it

it it it it

we we we we

we we we we

we we we we

we we we we

we we we we

we we we we

we we we we

we we we we

we we we we

he he he he

he he he he

he he he he

he he he he

he he he he

he he he he

he he he he

he he he he

he he he he

on on on on

on on on on

on on on on

on on on on

on on on on

on on on on

on on on on

on on on on

on on on on

on on on on

do do do do

do do do do

do do do do

do do do do

do do do do

do do do do

do do do do

do do do do

do do do do

me me me me

me me me me

me me me me

me me me me

me me me me

me me me me

me me me me

me me me me

me me me me

up up up up

up up up up

up up up up

up up up up

up up up up

up up up up

up up up up

up up up up

up up up up

go go go go

go go go go

go go go go

go go go go

go go go go

go go go go

go go go go

go go go go

go go go go

go go go go

us us us us

us us us us

us us us us

us us us us

us us us us

us us us us

us us us us

us us us us

us us us us

why why why why

why why why why

why why why why

why why why why

why why why why

why why why why

why why why why

why why why why

why why why why

how how how how

how how how how

how how how how

how how how how

how how how how

how how how how

how how how how

how how how how

how how how how

boy boy boy boy

boy boy boy boy

boy boy boy boy

boy boy boy boy

boy boy boy boy

boy boy boy boy

boy boy boy boy

boy boy boy boy

boy boy boy boy

buy buy buy buy

buy buy buy buy

buy buy buy buy

buy buy buy buy

buy buy buy buy

buy buy buy buy

buy buy buy buy

buy buy buy buy

buy buy buy buy

see see see see

see see see see

see see see see

see see see see

see see see see

see see see see

see see see see

see see see see

see see see see

see see see see

sea sea sea sea

sea sea sea sea

sea sea sea sea

sea sea sea sea

sea sea sea sea

sea sea sea sea

sea sea sea sea

sea sea sea sea

sea sea sea sea

saw saw saw saw

saw saw saw saw

saw saw saw saw

saw saw saw saw

saw saw saw saw

saw saw saw saw

saw saw saw saw

saw saw saw saw

saw saw saw saw

saw saw saw saw

pen pen pen pen

pen pen pen pen

pen pen pen pen

pen pen pen pen

pen pen pen pen

pen pen pen pen

pen pen pen pen

pen pen pen pen

pen pen pen pen

jug jug jug jug

jug jug jug jug

jug jug jug jug

jug jug jug jug

jug jug jug jug

jug jug jug jug

jug jug jug jug

jug jug jug jug

jug jug jug jug

van van van van

van van van van

van van van van

van van van van

van van van van

van van van van

van van van van

van van van van

van van van van

van van van van

zip zip zip zip

zip zip zip zip

zip zip zip zip

zip zip zip zip

zip zip zip zip

zip zip zip zip

zip zip zip zip

zip zip zip zip

zip zip zip zip

cat cat cat cat

cat cat cat cat

cat cat cat cat

cat cat cat cat

cat cat cat cat

cat cat cat cat

cat cat cat cat

cat cat cat cat

cat cat cat cat

dog dog dog dog

dog dog dog dog

dog dog dog dog

dog dog dog dog

dog dog dog dog

dog dog dog dog

dog dog dog dog

dog dog dog dog

dog dog dog dog

dog dog dog dog

pig pig pig pig

pig pig pig pig

pig pig pig pig

pig pig pig pig

pig pig pig pig

pig pig pig pig

pig pig pig pig

pig pig pig pig

pig pig pig pig

hen hen hen hen

hen hen hen hen

hen hen hen hen

hen hen hen hen

hen hen hen hen

hen hen hen hen

hen hen hen hen

hen hen hen hen

hen hen hen hen

hen hen hen hen

yam yam yam yam

yam yam yam yam

yam yam yam yam

yam yam yam yam

yam yam yam yam

yam yam yam yam

yam yam yam yam

yam yam yam yam

yam yam yam yam

war war war war

war war war war

war war war war

war war war war

war war war war

war war war war

war war war war

war war war war

war war war war

age age age age

age age age age

age age age age

age age age age

age age age age

age age age age

age age age age

age age age age

age age age age

pay pay pay pay

pay pay pay pay

pay pay pay pay

pay pay pay pay

pay pay pay pay

pay pay pay pay

pay pay pay pay

pay pay pay pay

pay pay pay pay

pay pay pay pay

map map map map

map map map map

map map map map

map map map map

map map map map

map map map map

map map map map

map map map map

map map map map

cop cop cop cop

cop cop cop cop

cop cop cop cop

cop cop cop cop

cop cop cop cop

cop cop cop cop

cop cop cop cop

cop cop cop cop

cop cop cop cop

file file file file file

file file file file file

file file file file file

file file file file file

file file file file file

file file file file file

file file file file file

file file file file file

file file file file file

file file file file file

able able able able

able able able able

able able able able

able able able able

able able able able

able able able able

able able able able

able able able able

able able able able

able able able able

army army army army

army army army army

army army army army

army army army army

army army army army

army army army army

army army army army

army army army army

army army army army

away away away away

away away away away

away away away away

away away away away

away away away away

away away away away

away away away away

away away away away

away away away away

away away away away

baby baby baby baby

baby baby baby baby

baby baby baby baby

baby baby baby baby

baby baby baby baby

baby baby baby baby

baby baby baby baby

baby baby baby baby

baby baby baby baby

ball ball ball ball

ball ball ball ball

ball ball ball ball

ball ball ball ball

ball ball ball ball

ball ball ball ball

ball ball ball ball

ball ball ball ball

ball ball ball ball

bank bank bank bank

bank bank bank bank

bank bank bank bank

bank bank bank bank

bank bank bank bank

bank bank bank bank

bank bank bank bank

bank bank bank bank

bank bank bank bank

bath bath bath bath

bath bath bath bath

bath bath bath bath

bath bath bath bath

bath bath bath bath

bath bath bath bath

bath bath bath bath

bath bath bath bath

bath bath bath bath

bell bell bell bell

bell bell bell bell

bell bell bell bell

bell bell bell bell

bell bell bell bell

bell bell bell bell

bell bell bell bell

bell bell bell bell

bell bell bell bell

bear bear bear bear

bear bear bear bear

bear bear bear bear

bear bear bear bear

bear bear bear bear

bear bear bear bear

bear bear bear bear

bear bear bear bear

bear bear bear bear

bear bear bear bear

belt belt belt belt

belt belt belt belt

belt belt belt belt

belt belt belt belt

belt belt belt belt

belt belt belt belt

belt belt belt belt

belt belt belt belt

belt belt belt belt

belt belt belt belt

beer beer beer beer

beer beer beer beer

beer beer beer beer

beer beer beer beer

beer beer beer beer

beer beer beer beer

beer beer beer beer

beer beer beer beer

beer beer beer beer

bird bird bird bird

bird bird bird bird

bird bird bird bird

bird bird bird bird

bird bird bird bird

bird bird bird bird

bird bird bird bird

bird bird bird bird

bird bird bird bird

bird bird bird bird

code code code code

code code code code

code code code code

code code code code

code code code code

code code code code

code code code code

code code code code

code code code code

code code code code

city city city city

city city city city

city city city city

city city city city

city city city city

city city city city

city city city city

city city city city

city city city city

cook cook cook cook

cook cook cook cook

cook cook cook cook

cook cook cook cook

cook cook cook cook

cook cook cook cook

cook cook cook cook

cook cook cook cook

cook cook cook cook

cook cook cook cook

date date date date

date date date date

date date date date

date date date date

date date date date

date date date date

date date date date

date date date date

date date date date

fire fire fire fire

fire fire fire fire

fire fire fire fire

fire fire fire fire

fire fire fire fire

fire fire fire fire

fire fire fire fire

fire fire fire fire

fire fire fire fire

dear dear dear dear

dear dear dear dear

dear dear dear dear

dear dear dear dear

dear dear dear dear

dear dear dear dear

dear dear dear dear

dear dear dear dear

dear dear dear dear

diet diet diet diet

diet diet diet diet

diet diet diet diet

diet diet diet diet

diet diet diet diet

diet diet diet diet

diet diet diet diet

diet diet diet diet

diet diet diet diet

east east east east

east east east east

east east east east

east east east east

east east east east

east east east east

east east east east

east east east east

east east east east

even even even even

even even even even

even even even even

even even even even

even even even even

even even even even

even even even even

even even even even

easy easy easy easy

easy easy easy easy

easy easy easy easy

easy easy easy easy

easy easy easy easy

easy easy easy easy

easy easy easy easy

easy easy easy easy

easy easy easy easy

easy easy easy easy

face face face face face

face face face face face

face face face face face

face face face face face

face face face face face

face face face face face

face face face face face

face face face face face

face face face face face

game game game game

game game game game

game game game game

game game game game

game game game game

game game game game

game game game game

game game game game

game game game game

grow grow grow grow

grow grow grow grow

grow grow grow grow

grow grow grow grow

grow grow grow grow

grow grow grow grow

grow grow grow grow

grow grow grow grow

grow grow grow grow

grow grow grow grow

hair hair hair hair

hair hair hair hair

hair hair hair hair

hair hair hair hair

hair hair hair hair

hair hair hair hair

hair hair hair hair

hair hair hair hair

hair hair hair hair

hard hard hard hard

hard hard hard hard

hard hard hard hard

hard hard hard hard

hard hard hard hard

hard hard hard hard

hard hard hard hard

hard hard hard hard

hard hard hard hard

head head head head

head head head head

head head head head

head head head head

head head head head

head head head head

head head head head

head head head head

head head head head

hero hero hero hero

hero hero hero hero

hero hero hero hero

hero hero hero hero

hero hero hero hero

hero hero hero hero

hero hero hero hero

hero hero hero hero

hero hero hero hero

high high high high

high high high high

high high high high

high high high high

high high high high

high high high high

high high high high

high high high high

high high high high

home home home home

home home home home

home home home home

home home home home

home home home home

home home home home

home home home home

home home home home

home home home home

iron iron iron iron

iron iron iron iron

iron iron iron iron

iron iron iron iron

iron iron iron iron

iron iron iron iron

iron iron iron iron

iron iron iron iron

iron iron iron iron

knee knee knee knee

knee knee knee knee

knee knee knee knee

knee knee knee knee

knee knee knee knee

knee knee knee knee

knee knee knee knee

knee knee knee knee

knee knee knee knee

knee knee knee knee

lack lack lack lack

lack lack lack lack

lack lack lack lack

lack lack lack lack

lack lack lack lack

lack lack lack lack

lack lack lack lack

lack lack lack lack

lack lack lack lack

lake lake lake lake

lake lake lake lake

lake lake lake lake

lake lake lake lake

lake lake lake lake

lake lake lake lake

lake lake lake lake

lake lake lake lake

lake lake lake lake

lead lead lead lead

lead lead lead lead

lead lead lead lead

lead lead lead lead

lead lead lead lead

lead lead lead lead

lead lead lead lead

lead lead lead lead

lead lead lead lead

lead lead lead lead

www.ingramcontent.com/pod-product-compliance
Lightning Source LLC
Chambersburg PA
CBHW081342160726
48000CB00010B/3195
9798558498707